USER'S GUIDE

FOR FENDER

TONE MASTER

PRO

Revealing the Strategies,Tips and Tricks for Mastering the Amp Guitar

Kevin Editions

Table Of Contents

Introduction

The Fender Tone Master Pro is a giant step forward in the guitar amplifier world as it marries state-of-the-art digital technology with the iconic tone and design aesthetics that have made Fender famous.

At its core, however, The Tone Master Pro is actually a digital modeling amp that accurately reproduces classic tube amps and effects pedals. On the other hand, The Tone Master Pro does not use analog circuitry or physical components to produce its unique sounds like traditional tube amplifiers; instead, it utilizes advanced digital signal processing to imitate vintage Fender amps' sonic characteristics as well as other renowned models by various makers.

One of the most impressive things about the Tone Master Pro is its flexibility. The Tone Master Pro offers an unmatched level of tonal versatility due to its wide variety of amp models and effects including vintage Fender tweed amps to modern high-gain monsters. Regardless if you are a bluesman hunting for creamy overdrive tones or a metal player searching for tight aggressive distortion, everything you need can be found in this exceptional piece.

Tone Master Pro design-wise has the Fender classic look with a black sleek housing, silver knobs, and the iconic red power light. The amp has intuitive controls that make it easy to get the tone you want and a large touchscreen display for a user-friendly interface. It also features a range of inputs/outputs including MIDI connectivity, stereo outputs, effects loops among others; making it useful in recording studios as well as live performances.

One of the most impressive things about this amp is its sound quality. Using advanced digital processing techniques alongside meticulous attention to detail by Fender, it produces superbly realistic tones that are equal or better than those offered by old-fashioned tube amps. Either when you raise the volume to play a loud solo or lower it to strum some smooth jazz chords, clarity, dynamics and warmth come through on Tone Master Pro with an effect which can satisfy even die-hard critics.

Its portability is another standout feature of the Tone Master Pro. The Tone Master Pro, unlike weighted tube amps that can be as heavy as 50 or more pounds, is light and handy hence ideal for live performers who need to move their equipment from one place to another one. Furthermore, the amp incorporates an inbuilt audio interface and Bluetooth functionality thus facilitating easy integration with recording software and mobile devices.

The Fender Tone Master Pro marks a true turning point in the history of guitar amplification technology. In terms of its fantastic sound quality, user-friendly design, and unmatched versatility, nothing beats the Tone Master Pro which sets a new benchmark for digital modeling amplifiers. If you are an experienced professional or just a weekend music lover then this amplifier will definitely make your imagination run wild and help you take your playing skills to a completely different level.

Chapter 1: Getting Started

Unboxing and Setup

When you unbox and set up your Fender Tone Master Pro, it is very interesting and not complicated at all, so that the guitarists will quickly start exploring its vast exercises and its original sound. In this section, we are going to look through how to unbox and set up the Tone Master Pro, so as to enable users to get their new amplifiers up and running.

The first step towards using the Tone Master Pro starts with a box opening experience. The packaging has been carefully designed by Fender to ensure that the amplifier reaches safely without any damage. Upon opening of the box one will find the Tone master pro safely tucked inside foam inserts along with other accessories like power cables, footswitches, user manuals among others.

After unpacking the amp, you may now go ahead and setup the Amp. It is made in a sleek design which is modern looking having black housing together with silver knobs on it as well as vivid touch screen displaying on top. Before switching on an amp it is necessary to check if any visible damages or faults are present in order for it to be delivered in good shape.

Users can then plug it into a power outlet with any of the available power cables when the Tone Master Pro is in the preferred position. It has a regular input jack for electric power, which will be compatible with most electrical outlets found in homes. When plugged, users then turn on the amplifier using its dedicated power switch located at its back.

Once this operation is done, there will be a vivid touch screen display welcoming you as you enter into the Tone Master Pro. This touchscreen display acts as the central point for controlling and customizing the settings of this amplifier. The interface is intuitive and user-friendly such that one can move through various menus and options effortlessly. Additionally, the amp comes loaded with several presets that are programmed in advance to facilitate initial exploration of its different tones and effects.

Other than a touch screen interface, Tone Master Pro also boasts physical controls like knobs and footswitches enabling a hands-on approach to essential parameter manipulations. Furthermore, these controls are receptive and tangible giving users an impression of traditional analog amplifiers they are used to operating.

Having powered on the amplifier and initialized the interface, users are now able to start experimenting with different amp models, effects and settings in order to come up with their preferred tone. The

Tone Master Pro offers an array of choices for any type of music or preference starting from a sought-after vintage Fender tube amp's warmth to a high-gain distortion pedal's modern aggressiveness.

The unboxing and setup process for the Fender Tone Master Pro is smooth and enjoyable thus setting the pace for hours of creative exploration and musical discovery. For guitarists seeking to unlock their full potential as well as unleash their creativity on stage, whether seasoned pros or novices, they will surely find inspiration in Tone Master Pro due its user-friendly interface, flexibility functions as well as exceptional sound quality.

Controls and Interface Overview

The Fender Tone Master Pro's controls and interface are designed so carefully that musicians can easily have a wide range of sounds and effects at their fingertips, all in one modern package. This part will look into the various controls and features that make up the Tone Master Pro's interface, as well as how they help users fine-tune their sound with accuracy and comfort.

At the core of the Tone Master Pro's interface is its lively touch screen display, which acts as a central control point for managing and configuring amplifier settings. The touch screen is responsive and easy to navigate through, allowing users to scroll down menus, adjust parameters, or select presets simply by swiping or tapping them on it. Whether you are equalizing the amplifier model or refining digital effect parameters on this unit, you will find this touch screen approach an unbroken user experience.

Moreover, this Tone Master Pro model contains physical controls such as knobs and footswitches as well, which are more satisfying as well because they give a person tactile feedback. For quicker access, these control panels surround the amplifiers casing making it easier to get around when performing live or in studios. The knobs do not wobble and are strongly made with precise adjustment qualities while the foot switches are also firm and quick to respond under any stage pressure.

The user interface of the Tone Master Pro has been developed for versatility and flexibility so that users can adjust their sound according to their individual tastes and musical genres. On its touchscreen display, amp models and effects can be easily chosen with an opportunity to recall saved presets quickly during performances or recording sessions. Furthermore, the amplifier has numerous connectivity options like MIDI, USB-C, Bluetooth etc., that allows integration of external appliances/software.

One of the most outstanding qualities of the Tone Master Pro's interface is that it is very simple and easy to use. The amplifier boasts state-of-the-art digital technology features, but its controls are straightforward and easily understood even by those who may be new in digital modeling. Regardless of your proficiency level, either being a beginner or a professional guitarist, you will find using this Tone Master Pro amp pretty simple thus enabling you to select a fitting tone for your music as well as come up with creative ways of playing the guitar.

The Fender Tone Master Pro control knobs and interface blend seamlessly in an example of how form meets function. From lush ambient soundscapes to searing lead tones to gritty blues riffs, the intuitive design and versatile controls on the Tone Master Pro make it extremely fun both onstage and in studio. With unmatched sound quality, outstanding build quality, and user friendly design, Fender has set a new precedent for what can be expected from digital modeling amplification.

Powering On and Basic Navigation

Switching on and navigating a Fender Tone Master Pro is easy to get users started with their amplifier swiftly. In this section, we will look at the process of switching on the Tone Master Pro and its user interface so that all its powerful features can be easily accessed by customers.

Firstly, users should check that the Tone Master Pro is connected to a power source with the provided power cord. The power input jack is located on the back panel of the amplifier, and one may simply plug in the cable into a regular electrical outlet to give it electricity. Following this connection, users can now change the position of the power switch to 'on' which is adjacent to the power input jack.

When powered up, Tone Master Pro's screen springs to life with an array of colors as it serves as a primary display for controlling and customizing settings. It has a responsive touch-screen display which guides navigation through menus; users can simply swipe or tap their finger buttons until they reach what they are looking for.

When the Tone Master Pro is powered up, it loads into its default preset most of the time, which gives users a starting point to begin playing immediately. This default preset may include a number of amp models, effects and settings that highlight the amp's capabilities and flexibility. They can now interact with digital buttons on the touchscreen display to change preamp models, set parameters, or customize their own sound.

Apart from the touchscreen display, there are other ways in which you can physically control your Tone Master Pro. For example, it comes equipped with knobs as well as footswitches that allow for hands-on manipulation of key parameters. These controls are spread throughout the amplifier's housing so they can be easily reached during any live performance or studio session performed on stage by a musician. On one hand, gain and tone controls can be adjusted using knobs while foot switches may also perform tasks such as deactivating or activating effects among others.

Its user interface is easy to navigate. So, you can easily enhance your sound using this device by just navigating through the menu or even scrolling using a touch of your fingering. The interface of this guitar amplifier has been made simple and less complex hence making it perfect for individuals who are new in the digital modeling technology.

Powering on and navigating the Fender Tone Master Pro is quick and easy because it provides a range of features and settings in one place. Regardless of whether you're fine-tuning effects, adjusting amp models or creating customized presets, the responsive touchscreen display together with physical controls that have tactile feel make it simple for users to get their desired tone during performances or studio sessions that lets creativity flow. With its straightforward layout and flexibility, the Tone Master Pro represents a new era for digital modeling amplifiers.

18

Chapter 2: Understanding Presets

Exploring Factory Presets

The Fender Tone Master Pro's factory presets provide a good starting point for users who want to access a wide range of tones, effects and amp models directly from the box. In this section we shall explore some of the factory presets available in the Tone Master Pro, and their various sonic landscapes that can stimulate creative sound development among its users.

When powered on for the first time, the Tone Master Pro presents factory settings as an indicator for how versatile it is. These settings are created by a team of sound designers and engineers at Fender, who have drawn inspiration from classic amps, iconic artists and contemporary music genres. Each preset has been carefully handpicked to give users an initial way into their own sonic investigations and hence give them a peek at what Tone Master Pro can do.

These factory defaults cut across a wide range of music genres and styles, ranging from clean tones of vintage Fender amps all the way to blistering high gain distortion for modern rock and metal. There are also presets based on legendary guitarists like Jimi Hendrix, Eric Clapton, Stevie Ray Vaughan and renowned amp models such as Fender Deluxe Reverb, Marshall Plexi, Vox AC30. Moreover, each preset often comes with an array of effects such as reverb, delay, chorus amongst others that gives users the possibility to experiment with different sounds as well as textures.

Thanks to the intuitive user interface of Tone Master Pro, navigating through factory presets is made simple. To scroll on available presets use left or right swipes on the touch-screen display then tap any desired preset instantly auditioned by listening to its sound. Once chosen, users can tinker with it by either adjusting parameters like gain/EQ/effects settings using physical controls or manipulating touchscreen interface.

One of the advantages of exploring the factory presets is that it enables users to quickly get accustomed with what the Tone Master Pro is capable of and also find some motivation for their own playing. The factory presets are a great collection for you to start with, whether you are new to tone-dialing or an experienced player looking for new sounds.

Apart from being a source of inspiration, the factory presets can be used as starting points when creating custom presets too. Users can modify a factory preset's settings and thereby make it sound different from anything else; then they can save these settings as custom preset so that they always have them by hand. This way, one could personalize his/her Tone Master Pro according to personal tastes and style of music thus ensuring that he/she will have an appropriate tone at any moment.

Exploring the factory presets on the Fender Tone Master Pro is an exhilarating experience that allows users to unlock the full potential of their amplifier. From vintage classics to modern marvels, the factory presets offer a diverse array of tones and effects to suit any musical style or preference. Whether you're a beginner or a seasoned pro, the factory presets provide a solid foundation for your sonic explorations and inspire you to push the boundaries of your creativity.

Creating and Saving Custom Presets

Creating and saving custom presets on the Fender Tone Master Pro is a powerful feature that allows users to tailor their amplifier to their own unique preferences and playing style. Let's explore the process of creating and saving custom presets on the Tone Master Pro, as well as how this feature empowers users to craft their ideal tone with precision and ease.

To begin creating a custom preset, users can start by selecting an existing factory preset as a starting point. Once they have found a preset that they like, they can begin making adjustments to the various parameters such as amp model, EQ settings, effects, and more. These adjustments can be made using the Tone Master Pro's intuitive touchscreen interface, allowing users to easily dial in their desired sound with just a few taps and swipes.

One of the key features of the Tone Master Pro is its ability to save custom presets for quick recall later on. Once users have dialed in their desired settings, they can save their custom preset to one of the amplifier's available preset slots. This allows them to easily access their custom tone at any time, without having to manually adjust the settings each time they want to use it.

In addition to saving custom presets directly on the Tone Master Pro, users can also save and organize presets using external devices such as computers or smartphones. The amplifier features USB-C connectivity, allowing users to connect it to their computer and use the Tone Master Pro Editor software to manage and organize their presets. This software provides a visual interface for creating, editing, and organizing presets, making it easy for users to create and save custom tones to suit their specific needs.

Creating and saving custom presets on the Tone Master Pro is not only convenient, but it also allows users to experiment and explore new sounds with ease. Whether you're looking to recreate the tone of your favorite guitarist, dial in the perfect sound for a specific song or genre, or simply explore new sonic possibilities, the ability to create and save custom presets gives you the flexibility and control to sculpt your ideal tone.

Another benefit of creating custom presets is the ability to share them with others. Whether you're collaborating with other musicians, teaching guitar lessons, or simply sharing your favorite tones with friends, the ability to save and share custom presets allows you to easily exchange ideas and inspiration with others. This fosters a sense of community and collaboration among Tone Master Pro users, as they can learn from each other's creations and build upon them to create new and exciting sounds.

Creating and saving custom presets on the Fender Tone Master Pro is a powerful feature that empowers users to craft their ideal tone with precision and ease. Whether you're a beginner or a seasoned pro, the ability to create and save custom presets allows you to tailor the Tone Master Pro to your own unique preferences and playing style, unlocking a world of sonic possibilities in the process. With its intuitive interface, versatile features, and seamless connectivity options, the Tone Master Pro is the ultimate tool for guitarists looking to express themselves creatively and push the boundaries of their playing.

Managing Presets

Managing presets on the Fender Tone Master Pro is an essential aspect of maximizing the amplifier's potential and ensuring that users can access their favorite tones quickly and easily. In this part, we'll explore the various tools and techniques available for managing presets on the Tone Master Pro, as well as how users can organize, edit, and customize their presets to suit their specific needs.

One of the primary ways to manage presets on the Tone Master Pro is through the amplifier's touchscreen interface. The touchscreen display provides users with an intuitive and user-friendly interface for browsing, selecting, and editing presets. Users can scroll through the available presets using simple swipe gestures, tap on individual presets to audition them, and make adjustments to the settings using on-screen controls. Additionally, users can organize their presets into folders or categories, making it easy to group similar presets together for quick access.

In addition to managing presets directly on the amplifier, users can also use external devices such as computers or smartphones to manage their presets. The Tone Master Pro features USB-C connectivity, allowing users to connect it to their computer and use the Tone Master Pro Editor software to manage and organize their presets. This software provides a visual interface for creating, editing, and organizing presets, making it easy for users to organize their presets and create custom presets from scratch.

One of the key features of the Tone Master Pro's preset management system is its ability to save presets to external storage devices such as USB flash drives or SD cards. This allows users to easily transfer presets between different amplifiers, share presets with other users, or back up their presets for safekeeping. Additionally, users can import and export presets in a variety of formats, making it easy to share presets with friends, collaborate with other musicians, or download presets from online communities.

Another important aspect of managing presets on the Tone Master Pro is the ability to customize and edit existing presets to suit your specific needs. Users can adjust parameters such as amp model, EQ settings, effects, and more, allowing them to tailor each preset to their own unique preferences and playing style. Additionally, users can rename presets, assign them to specific footswitches for quick access, and reorder them to prioritize their favorite presets.

The ability to manage presets on the Tone Master Pro gives users the flexibility and control to tailor their amplifier to their own unique preferences and playing style. Whether you're a gigging musician looking to organize your presets for easy access on stage, a recording artist seeking to create custom tones for studio sessions, or a hobbyist guitarist exploring new sonic possibilities, the Tone Master Pro's preset management system provides the tools and flexibility you need to take your playing to the next level.

Chapter 3: Navigating the Interface

Touchscreen Functionality

The touchscreen functionality of the Fender Tone Master Pro is a standout feature that enhances the user experience and provides intuitive control over the amplifier's settings and parameters. Let's take a look at the various ways in which the touchscreen display enhances the usability of the Tone Master Pro, as well as how users can take advantage of its features to craft their ideal tone with precision and ease.

The touchscreen display on the Tone Master Pro serves as the central hub for controlling and customizing the amplifier's settings. Measuring 7 inches diagonally, the touchscreen provides ample space for displaying detailed information and graphical representations of amp models, effects, and settings. The display is bright, vibrant, and responsive to touch, allowing users to navigate menus, adjust parameters, and select presets with ease.

One of the key benefits of the touchscreen functionality is its intuitive nature, which allows users to interact with the amplifier in a way that feels natural and intuitive. Whether you're adjusting the EQ settings of your amp model, tweaking the parameters of a digital effect, or selecting a preset from the library, the touchscreen interface provides a seamless and intuitive user experience that makes it easy to dial in your desired tone.

The touchscreen display also offers multi-touch support, allowing users to perform gestures such as pinch-to-zoom and swipe-to-scroll to navigate menus and interact with on-screen controls. This makes it easy to zoom in on specific parameters for fine-tuning, scroll through lists of presets or effects, and perform other actions that require precise control.

In addition to controlling individual parameters and settings, the touchscreen display also provides visual feedback and information about the current state of the amplifier. For example, when adjusting the EQ settings of an amp model, users can see a graphical representation of the frequency response curve, allowing them to see how their adjustments affect the overall tone of the amplifier.

Another useful feature of the touchscreen display is its ability to display detailed information about amp models, effects, and settings. When selecting a preset or adjusting a parameter, users can see information such as the name of the amp model or effect, its settings and parameters, and any other relevant information. This makes it easy to understand how different settings and parameters affect the overall sound of the amplifier, allowing users to make informed decisions when crafting their tone.

Overall, the touchscreen functionality of the Fender Tone Master Pro enhances the user experience and provides intuitive control over the amplifier's settings and parameters. Whether you're a beginner or a seasoned pro, the touchscreen interface makes it easy to dial in your desired tone with precision and ease, allowing you to unlock the full potential of the Tone Master Pro and take your playing to the next level.

Using Foot Switches and Knobs

Using foot switches and knobs on the Fender Tone Master Pro is an integral part of controlling and shaping your guitar tone with precision and flexibility. Let's see how these physical controls enhance the user experience, provide tactile feedback, and allow for hands-on manipulation of key parameters.

The Tone Master Pro features a set of foot switches and knobs strategically placed around the amplifier's housing, allowing for easy access and control during live performances or studio sessions. These physical controls offer tactile feedback and responsiveness, giving users a sense of familiarity and control reminiscent of traditional analog amplifiers.

The foot switches on the Tone Master Pro serve multiple functions, allowing users to activate or bypass effects, switch between presets, control the built-in looper, and more. Each foot switch is programmable, meaning users can assign it to perform a specific function or trigger a particular action, giving them the flexibility to tailor the amplifier's operation to their own individual preferences and playing style.

In addition to the foot switches, the Tone Master Pro also features a set of knobs that allow for hands-on manipulation of key parameters such as gain, tone, volume, and effects levels. These knobs are sturdy and well-built, with smooth rotation and precise adjustment, allowing users to dial in their desired tone with ease and accuracy.

One of the key benefits of using foot switches and knobs on the Tone Master Pro is their versatility and flexibility. Whether you're performing on stage, recording in the studio, or practicing at home, these physical controls give you the ability to shape your tone in real-time, responding to the dynamics of your playing and the needs of the music.

For example, during a live performance, you might use the foot switches to switch between clean and distorted tones, activate a solo boost, or engage a delay effect for added depth and texture. Meanwhile, the knobs can be used to adjust the EQ settings of your amp model, tweak the parameters of your effects, or fine-tune the overall volume and balance of your sound.

In addition to their practical functionality, using foot switches and knobs on the Tone Master Pro also adds a tactile element to the user experience, enhancing the sense of connection between the player and the amplifier. Whether you're stomping on a foot switch to engage a powerful distortion pedal or twisting a knob to dial in the perfect amount of reverb, these physical controls give you a sense of agency and control over your sound, empowering you to express yourself creatively and dynamically.

Using foot switches and knobs on the Fender Tone Master Pro is an essential aspect of controlling and shaping your guitar tone with precision and flexibility. Whether you're performing on stage, recording in the studio, or practicing at home, these physical controls give you the ability to shape your sound in real-time, responding to the needs of the music and expressing yourself creatively. With their tactile feedback and versatile functionality, foot switches and knobs add a level of depth and immersion to the user experience, enhancing the sense of connection between the player and the amplifier.

Chapter 4: Exploring Amp Models and Effects

The Fender Tone Master Pro boasts an impressive array of amp models, meticulously crafted to replicate the iconic tones of some of the most legendary amplifiers in history. In this section, we'll take a comprehensive look at the available amp models on the Tone Master Pro, exploring their characteristics, tonal qualities, and historical significance.

Fender Deluxe Reverb: The Deluxe Reverb is a classic Fender amplifier known for its sparkling clean tones and lush spring reverb. It has been a staple of countless recordings and live performances since its introduction in the 1960s, prized for its warm and dynamic sound.

Fender Bassman: The Bassman is another iconic Fender amplifier that has left an indelible mark on the world of guitar tone. Originally designed as a bass amplifier, the Bassman quickly gained popularity among guitarists for its rich, full-bodied sound and creamy overdrive tones.

Marshall Plexi: The Marshall Plexi is a legendary amplifier that played a pivotal role in shaping the sound of rock music in the 1960s and 70s. Known for its raw, aggressive tone and singing sustain, the Plexi is favored by guitarists seeking a classic rock sound with plenty of bite and attitude.

Vox AC30: The Vox AC30 is a British classic renowned for its chimey cleans and distinctive jangly tone. Used by countless artists from The Beatles to The Edge, the AC30 delivers a bright and articulate sound that cuts through the mix with ease.

Fender Tweed: The Tweed series of amplifiers from Fender represents the company's early forays into guitar amplification, characterized by their rugged construction and warm, vintage tone. These amps are beloved for their gritty overdrive and fat, punchy midrange.

Each amp model on the Tone Master Pro is meticulously crafted to replicate the unique characteristics and tonal nuances of its real-world counterpart. From the sparkling cleans of the Deluxe Reverb to the raucous overdrive of the Marshall Plexi, each model captures the essence of the original amplifier, allowing users to dial in authentic vintage tones with ease.

In addition to the classic Fender and Marshall models, the Tone Master Pro also offers a selection of modern high-gain amp models for players seeking a more aggressive sound. These models deliver tight, saturated distortion with plenty of punch and clarity, making them ideal for genres such as metal and hard rock.

One of the standout features of the Tone Master Pro is its ability to seamlessly switch between different amp models with the touch of a button, allowing users to explore a wide range of tones and textures without having to switch amps or pedals. This versatility makes the Tone Master Pro a powerful tool for both live performance and studio recording, allowing users to quickly dial in the perfect tone for any musical situation.

The Fender Tone Master Pro offers an impressive selection of amp models that faithfully capture the essence of some of the most iconic amplifiers in history. From the classic Fender clean tones to the aggressive distortion of the Marshall Plexi, each model provides a unique sonic palette for users to explore and express themselves creatively. With its versatile functionality and authentic vintage tones, the Tone Master Pro is a powerhouse amplifier that delivers exceptional sound quality and performance in a compact and convenient package.

Understanding Built-in Effects

Understanding the built-in effects of the Fender Tone Master Pro is essential for unlocking the full potential of the amplifier and crafting your desired guitar tone. In this part, we are going to explore the range of effects available on the Tone Master Pro, including reverb, delay, modulation, and more, and discuss how each effect can be used to shape your sound and enhance your playing experience.

Reverb: Reverb is a staple effect in the world of guitar tone, adding depth, dimension, and ambiance to your sound. The Tone Master Pro offers a selection of high-quality reverb algorithms, including spring, hall, plate, and room, each with its own unique character and tonal qualities. Whether you're looking to add a subtle touch of ambience to your clean tones or create lush, atmospheric textures, the built-in reverb effects of the Tone Master Pro have you covered.

Delay: Delay is another essential effect that can add depth and richness to your guitar tone. The Tone Master Pro features a variety of delay effects, including analog, digital, tape, and reverse delays, each with its own distinctive sound and character. From classic slapback echoes to swirling, atmospheric trails, the built-in delay effects of the Tone Master Pro allow you to create a wide range of dynamic and expressive sounds.

Modulation: Modulation effects such as chorus, flanger, and phaser can add movement and texture to your guitar tone, giving it a sense of depth and dimension. The Tone Master Pro offers a selection of modulation effects that allow you to experiment with different modulation rates, depths, and intensities, allowing you to dial in everything from subtle, shimmering chorus to swirling, psychedelic textures.

Overdrive and Distortion: The Tone Master Pro also features a selection of overdrive and distortion effects that allow you to add grit, crunch, and saturation to your guitar tone. Whether you're looking for a smooth, creamy overdrive or a raucous, aggressive distortion, the built-in overdrive and distortion effects of the Tone Master Pro provide a wide range of tonal options to suit any musical style or genre.

Wah and EQ: Additionally, the Tone Master Pro offers a selection of other effects and processing tools, including wah-wah, EQ, and compression. These effects allow you to further shape and sculpt your guitar tone, giving you the ability to boost frequencies, shape dynamics, and add expressive filtering effects to your sound.

One of the key benefits of the built-in effects of the Tone Master Pro is their seamless integration with the amplifier's other features and controls. Whether you're adjusting the parameters of an effect using the touchscreen display, assigning effects to footswitches for hands-free control, or fine-tuning settings using the physical knobs, the built-in effects of the Tone Master Pro are designed to be intuitive and easy to use, allowing you to focus on your playing and creativity without getting bogged down in technical details.

Adjusting Amp and Effect Parameters

Adjusting amp and effect parameters on the Fender Tone Master Pro is a crucial aspect of tailoring your guitar tone to suit your preferences and musical style. Let's highlights the various parameters that can be adjusted on the Tone Master Pro, including amp settings, EQ controls, and effect parameters, and discuss how each parameter affects the overall sound of the amplifier.

Amp Settings: The Tone Master Pro offers a wide range of amp settings that allow you to customize the characteristics of your amp model to achieve your desired tone. These settings typically include controls for gain, volume, treble, middle, bass, and presence, allowing you to shape the frequency response, dynamics, and overall character of your sound. Adjusting the gain control, for example, allows you to control the amount of overdrive or distortion in your tone, while adjusting the EQ controls allows you to shape the tonal balance and timbre of your sound.

EQ Controls: In addition to the amp settings, the Tone Master Pro also features a set of EQ controls that allow you to further shape and sculpt your guitar tone. These controls typically include knobs for adjusting the bass, midrange, and treble frequencies, as well as a presence control for adding sparkle and definition to your sound. By adjusting these EQ controls, you can tailor the frequency response of your amplifier to suit the specific characteristics of your guitar, playing style, and musical genre.

Effect Parameters: The Tone Master Pro offers a variety of built-in effects, including reverb, delay, modulation, and more, each with its own set of parameters that can be adjusted to customize the sound and behavior of the effect. For example, the reverb effect may include parameters such as decay time, pre-delay, diffusion, and damping, allowing you to adjust the size, shape, and character of the reverb effect to suit your preferences. Similarly, the delay effect may include parameters such as delay time, feedback, and modulation depth, allowing you to create a wide range of delay effects, from subtle echoes to swirling, atmospheric trails.

Touchscreen Interface: Adjusting amp and effect parameters on the Tone Master Pro is made easy thanks to its intuitive touchscreen interface. The touchscreen display provides a graphical representation of the various parameters and settings, allowing you to easily navigate menus, select presets, and adjust settings with just a few taps and swipes. Whether you're adjusting the gain on your amp model, tweaking the EQ settings, or dialing in the perfect delay effect, the touchscreen interface makes it easy to fine-tune your sound and create your ideal tone.

Foot Switches and Knobs: In addition to the touchscreen interface, the Tone Master Pro also features physical controls such as foot switches and knobs that allow for hands-on manipulation of key parameters. The footswitches can be assigned to control various functions and effects, allowing you to switch between presets, engage or bypass effects, and control the built-in looper with ease. Meanwhile, the knobs provide tactile feedback and precise control over parameters such as gain, volume, and EQ, allowing you to dial in your desired tone with precision and accuracy.

Adjusting amp and effect parameters on the Fender Tone Master Pro is a straightforward process that allows you to tailor your guitar tone to suit your preferences and musical style. Whether you're adjusting amp settings, EQ controls, or effect parameters, the Tone Master Pro provides a wide range of options for customizing your sound and expressing yourself creatively on the guitar. With its intuitive touchscreen interface, hands-on controls, and versatile features, the Tone Master Pro makes it easy to dial in your perfect tone and unleash your musical potential.

Chapter 5: Advanced Features

Utilizing the Audio Interface

Utilizing the audio interface of the Fender Tone Master Pro opens up a world of possibilities for recording, performing, and practicing with your guitar. Here, we explored the various features and capabilities of the Tone Master Pro's audio interface, including its connectivity options, recording capabilities, and integration with digital audio workstations (DAWs).

Connectivity Options: The Tone Master Pro features a comprehensive array of connectivity options, allowing you to connect to a wide range of devices and peripherals. These include stereo outputs in both quarter-inch and XLR formats, allowing you to connect directly to a mixer, audio interface, or PA system for live performance or recording. Additionally, the Tone Master Pro features multiple effects sends and returns, two expression pedal outlets, a mic/line and instrument input, headphone output, MIDI in and out, USB-C, MicroSD, and Bluetooth connectivity. This extensive connectivity ensures that you can integrate the Tone Master Pro seamlessly into your existing setup, whether you're recording in the studio, performing live on stage, or practicing at home.

Recording Capabilities: The audio interface of the Tone Master Pro allows you to record high-quality audio directly to your computer or digital audio workstation (DAW) without the need for additional hardware. Simply connect the Tone Master Pro to your computer via USB-C, and you can record your guitar directly into your DAW with pristine sound quality and minimal latency. This makes it easy to capture your performances, ideas, and musical creations with professional-quality sound, whether you're tracking guitar parts for a song, recording demos, or laying down tracks for a full-length album.

Integration with DAWs: The Tone Master Pro's audio interface is compatible with a wide range of digital audio workstations (DAWs), including popular software such as Pro Tools, Logic Pro, Ableton Live, and GarageBand. This allows you to seamlessly integrate the Tone Master Pro into your existing recording setup and take advantage of its powerful amp modeling and effects processing capabilities within your DAW environment. Whether you're recording guitar parts, programming MIDI tracks, or mixing and mastering your final mix, the Tone Master Pro's audio interface provides the flexibility and versatility you need to bring your musical ideas to life.

Direct Monitoring: One of the key features of the Tone Master Pro's audio interface is its direct monitoring capability, which allows you to monitor your guitar signal with zero latency while recording. This means that you can hear your guitar signal in real-time as you play, without any delay or lag, making it easier to stay in sync with your backing tracks and capture your best performances. Direct monitoring also allows you to hear the effects processing applied to your guitar signal in real-time, giving you instant feedback and control over your tone as you play.

Headphone Output: The Tone Master Pro's headphone output allows you to monitor your guitar signal privately and discreetly, making it ideal for practicing at home or recording late at night without disturbing others. The headphone output delivers high-quality audio with plenty of volume and clarity, allowing you to hear every nuance of your guitar tone with precision and detail. Whether you're practicing scales, learning new songs, or recording guitar parts, the headphone output of the Tone Master Pro provides a convenient and immersive listening experience.

The audio interface of the Fender Tone Master Pro is a powerful tool that allows you to record, perform, and practice with your guitar with professional-quality sound and versatility. With its extensive connectivity options, recording capabilities, integration with DAWs, direct monitoring, and headphone output, the Tone Master Pro's audio interface provides everything you need to unleash your creativity and express yourself musically, whether you're recording in the studio, performing live on stage, or practicing at home.

Incorporating External Pedals and Effects

Incorporating external pedals and effects into the Fender Tone Master Pro setup expands its sonic capabilities and allows for further customization of your guitar tone. Here, we'll explore how you can seamlessly integrate external pedals and effects with the Tone Master Pro, enhancing your sound and unlocking new creative possibilities.

Compatibility: One of the advantages of the Tone Master Pro is its compatibility with a wide range of external pedals and effects. Whether you prefer analog stompboxes, digital multi-effects units, or boutique pedals, the Tone Master Pro's flexible connectivity options allow you to incorporate them into your setup with ease. Simply connect your pedals to the Tone Master Pro's effects loops or input jacks, and you can instantly expand your sonic palette with additional effects, textures, and tones.

Effects Loops: The Tone Master Pro features multiple effects loops, allowing you to integrate external pedals and effects into your signal chain with precision and flexibility. Effects loops are especially useful for time-based effects such as delay and reverb, as they allow you to place them in parallel with your amp's preamp and power amp sections, preserving the integrity of your guitar tone while adding depth and dimension to your sound. Additionally, effects loops can be used to incorporate external modulation, distortion, and other effects pedals into your setup, giving you complete control over your signal chain and allowing you to create complex, layered tones with ease.

Integration: Integrating external pedals and effects into the Tone Master Pro setup is a straightforward process that allows you to tailor your guitar tone to suit your preferences and musical style. Whether you're looking to add subtle touches of modulation and ambience or create bold, dynamic textures and effects, the Tone Master Pro's flexible connectivity options make it easy to incorporate external pedals and effects into your signal chain and experiment with different combinations and settings to achieve your desired sound.

Tone Sculpting: External pedals and effects can be used to further sculpt and shape your guitar tone, allowing you to fine-tune your sound and achieve the perfect balance of clarity, dynamics, and expression. For example, you can use EQ pedals to boost or cut specific frequencies, giving you greater control over the tonal balance and character of your sound. Similarly, you can use distortion, overdrive, and fuzz pedals to add grit, crunch, and saturation to your tone, creating rich, harmonically complex textures and timbres that cut through the mix and grab the listener's attention.

Creative Expression: Incorporating external pedals and effects into your Tone Master Pro setup opens up a world of creative possibilities, allowing you to experiment with different sounds, textures, and effects to create unique and expressive guitar tones. Whether you're crafting lush, ambient soundscapes, laying down blistering solos, or driving the rhythm with crunchy, aggressive distortion, external pedals and effects give you the tools you need to express yourself creatively and push the boundaries of your playing.

Incorporating external pedals and effects into the Fender Tone Master Pro setup enhances its sonic capabilities and allows for further customization of your guitar tone. Whether you're looking to add subtle touches of modulation and ambience or create bold, dynamic textures and effects, external pedals and effects give you the flexibility and versatility to shape your sound and express yourself creatively. With its flexible connectivity options, integration with effects loops, and compatibility with a wide range of pedals and effects, the Tone Master Pro provides everything you need to take your guitar tone to the next level and unleash your creativity on stage and in the studio.

Microphone and Cabinet Modeling Options

Exploring microphone and cabinet modeling options on the Fender Tone Master Pro opens up a world of possibilities for shaping and refining your guitar tone. Let's explore the various microphone and cabinet modeling options available on the Tone Master Pro, discussing how they work and how you can use them to achieve your desired sound.

Mic and Cabinet Modeling: The Tone Master Pro offers a wide range of microphone and cabinet modeling options that allow you to emulate the sound of classic amplifiers and speaker cabinets with stunning accuracy and realism. These modeling options are based on extensive research and analysis of the characteristics of vintage microphones and speaker cabinets, allowing you to capture the essence of iconic guitar tones from the past and recreate them in your own playing.

Virtual Mic Placement: One of the key features of the Tone Master Pro's mic and cabinet modeling options is the ability to adjust virtual mic placement, allowing you to fine-tune the position of the microphone relative to the speaker cone and achieve the perfect balance of warmth, clarity, and presence in your guitar tone. Whether you prefer the close-miked sound of a dynamic microphone or the spacious ambience of a room mic, the Tone Master Pro's virtual mic placement controls give you the flexibility to experiment with different mic positions and find the perfect sound for your playing style and musical genre.

Speaker Cabinet Selection: In addition to virtual mic placement, the Tone Master Pro also allows you to select from a variety of speaker cabinet options, each with its own unique tonal characteristics and sonic qualities. Whether you prefer the punchy midrange and tight low end of a closed-back cabinet or the airy openness and extended low end of an open-back cabinet, the Tone Master Pro's speaker cabinet selection allows you to tailor your guitar tone to suit your preferences and achieve the perfect balance of clarity, warmth, and definition.

Tonal Versatility: The microphone and cabinet modeling options on the Tone Master Pro provide a level of tonal versatility and flexibility that is unmatched by traditional guitar amplifiers. With the ability to emulate the sound of vintage Fender, Marshall, Vox, and other iconic amplifiers and speaker cabinets, the Tone Master Pro allows you to explore a wide range of sonic textures and timbres, from sparkling cleans and creamy overdrives to gritty distortions and searing lead tones. Whether you're playing blues, rock, jazz, country, or metal, the Tone Master Pro's microphone and cabinet modeling options give you the tools you need to dial in your perfect tone and express yourself creatively on the guitar.

Recording and Performance: The microphone and cabinet modeling options on the Tone Master Pro are not only great for live performance but also for recording in the studio. By capturing the sound of vintage microphones and speaker cabinets with stunning accuracy and realism, the Tone Master Pro allows you to achieve professional-quality guitar tones without the need for expensive recording gear or elaborate mic setups. Whether you're tracking guitar parts for a song, recording demos, or laying down tracks for a full-length album, the Tone Master Pro's microphone and cabinet modeling options provide everything you need to capture the perfect tone and bring your musical ideas to life.

Exploring microphone and cabinet modeling options on the Fender Tone Master Pro opens up a world of possibilities for shaping and refining your guitar tone. With virtual mic placement, speaker cabinet selection, and tonal versatility, the Tone Master Pro allows you to achieve professional-quality guitar tones with stunning accuracy and realism, whether you're playing live on stage or recording in the studio. Whether you're a blues guitarist, a rock guitarist, a jazz guitarist, or a metal guitarist, the Tone Master Pro's microphone and cabinet modeling options provide the tools you need to unlock your full creative potential and express yourself musically on the guitar.

54

Chapter 6: Performance and Recording

Using the Tone Master Pro Live on Stage

Using the Tone Master Pro live on stage offers guitarists a versatile and reliable solution for delivering exceptional tone in a variety of performance settings. In this part, we'll explore how the Tone Master Pro can be effectively used in a live performance scenario, covering setup, sound optimization, and performance techniques.

Setup: Setting up the Tone Master Pro for live performance is straightforward and intuitive. Begin by connecting your guitar to the input jack of the Tone Master Pro and connecting the amp to the venue's sound system or speaker cabinets using the appropriate outputs, whether quarter-inch, XLR, or a combination of both. Ensure that all cables are securely connected and that the amp is powered on and ready to go. Additionally, consider using a reliable power conditioner to protect the amp from electrical interference and ensure consistent performance throughout the show.

Sound Optimization: Once the Tone Master Pro is set up, take some time to optimize your guitar tone for the venue and performance context. Experiment with different amp models, effects settings, and EQ adjustments to dial in your desired sound, taking into account factors such as room acoustics, stage volume, and band dynamics. Use the built-in presets and customizable settings of the Tone Master Pro to create tailored sounds for different songs and performance scenarios, ensuring that your tone cuts through the mix and complements the rest of the band.

Performance Techniques: When using the Tone Master Pro live on stage, it's important to consider performance techniques that can enhance your playing and engage the audience. Experiment with dynamic playing techniques such as palm muting, fingerpicking, and alternate picking to create expressive and emotive performances. Use the Tone Master Pro's footswitches and expression pedal inputs to control effects, amp settings, and performance features such as volume swells and wah effects, allowing you to add depth and dimension to your sound in real-time.

Stage Presence: In addition to sound optimization and performance techniques, stage presence plays a crucial role in delivering a memorable live performance with the Tone Master Pro. Engage with the audience, make eye contact, and move around the stage with confidence and energy, conveying passion and emotion through your playing. Use stage lighting and visual effects to enhance the mood and atmosphere of your performance, creating a captivating and immersive experience for the audience.

Interacting with Other Musicians: When performing live with the Tone Master Pro, it's important to interact effectively with other musicians on stage to ensure a cohesive and professional performance. Communicate with your bandmates through visual cues, verbal cues, and musical cues, staying in sync with the rhythm, tempo, and dynamics of the music. Listen attentively to the other instruments and adjust your playing accordingly, supporting the overall sound and vibe of the band.

Using the Tone Master Pro live on stage offers guitarists a versatile and reliable solution for delivering exceptional tone in a variety of performance settings. By following the steps outlined in this section, including setup, sound optimization, performance techniques, stage presence, and interacting with other musicians, you can harness the full potential of the Tone Master Pro and deliver memorable and captivating live performances that leave a lasting impression on your audience. Whether you're playing in a small club, a large concert hall, or an outdoor festival stage, the Tone Master Pro provides everything you need to shine as a guitarist and musician.

Recording With the Tone Master Pro in the Studio

Recording with the Tone Master Pro in the studio opens up a world of possibilities for capturing professional-quality guitar tones with ease and precision. Let's look at how the Tone Master Pro can be effectively used in a studio recording environment, covering setup, signal routing, tone shaping, and recording techniques.

Setup: Setting up the Tone Master Pro for studio recording is straightforward and flexible. Begin by connecting your guitar to the input jack of the Tone Master Pro and connecting the amp to your recording interface or mixer using the appropriate outputs, whether quarter-inch, XLR, or a combination of both. Ensure that all cables are securely connected and that the amp is powered on and ready to go. Consider placing the Tone Master Pro in an isolated area of the studio to minimize bleed from other instruments and ensure clean recordings.

Signal Routing: The Tone Master Pro offers a variety of signal routing options that allow you to capture professional-quality guitar tones with ease and precision. Experiment with different amp models, effects settings, and EQ adjustments to dial in your desired sound, taking advantage of the Tone Master Pro's built-in presets and customizable settings to create tailored tones for different songs and recording scenarios. Use the Tone Master Pro's stereo outputs, effects loops, and headphone output to route your guitar signal to the recording interface or mixer, ensuring optimal signal flow and sound quality throughout the recording process.

Tone Shaping: Once the Tone Master Pro is set up and connected to your recording interface or mixer, take some time to shape and refine your guitar tone for the recording session. Experiment with different amp models, cabinet simulations, and microphone placements to achieve the perfect balance of warmth, clarity, and presence in your tone. Use the Tone Master Pro's EQ controls, effects settings, and tone shaping tools to sculpt your sound to perfection, ensuring that your guitar tone sits comfortably in the mix and complements the other instruments in the arrangement.

Recording Techniques: When recording with the Tone Master Pro in the studio, consider employing a variety of recording techniques to capture the best possible sound. Experiment with different microphone placements, room acoustics, and recording setups to find the perfect sound for your guitar tone. Consider using multiple microphones and blending them together in the mix to capture the full spectrum of your guitar's sound, from sparkling highs to thunderous lows. Use techniques such as close miking, room miking, and stereo miking to capture different aspects of your guitar tone and create depth and dimension in your recordings.

Post-Production: After recording with the Tone Master Pro, take some time to review and edit your recordings to ensure that they meet your expectations. Use digital audio workstation (DAW) software to clean up any noise or artifacts in the recordings, adjust levels and EQ settings, and add additional effects and processing to enhance your guitar tone. Experiment with different mixing techniques, panning strategies, and mastering settings to achieve the perfect balance and clarity in your final mix, ensuring that your guitar tone shines through with clarity and definition.

Recording with the Tone Master Pro in the studio offers guitarists a versatile and powerful tool for capturing professional-quality guitar tones with ease and precision. By following the steps outlined in this section, including setup, signal routing, tone shaping, recording techniques, and post-production, you can harness the full potential of the Tone Master Pro and create stunning recordings that showcase your guitar playing and musical creativity. Whether you're recording demos, laying down tracks for an album, or producing music for film and television, the Tone Master Pro provides everything you need to achieve professional-quality results and bring your musical ideas to life.

Tips for Optimal Performance and Recording Quality

Achieving optimal performance and recording quality with the Tone Master Pro requires attention to detail, experimentation, and an understanding of the amp's capabilities. In this section, we highlighted several tips to help you get the most out of your Tone Master Pro in both live performance and studio recording settings.

1. Experiment with Amp Models and Effects: The Tone Master Pro offers a wide range of amp models and built-in effects, allowing you to dial in a variety of tones to suit different musical styles and performance contexts. Take the time to experiment with different amp models, effects combinations, and settings to discover new sounds and textures that complement your playing style.

2. Customize Your Presets: Utilize the Tone Master Pro's preset functionality to save and recall your favorite amp and effects settings for different songs and performance scenarios. Customize your presets to match the specific requirements of each song, adjusting parameters such as gain, EQ, reverb, and

delay to achieve the perfect tone for each musical passage.

3. Fine-Tune Your EQ: Pay attention to the EQ settings on the Tone Master Pro to ensure that your guitar tone sits well in the mix and cuts through during live performances and studio recordings. Experiment with different EQ settings to boost or cut specific frequencies, shaping your tone to fit the musical context and achieve optimal clarity and balance.

4. Optimize Your Signal Chain: Consider the order in which you connect your pedals and effects to the Tone Master Pro to achieve the best possible sound quality and performance. Experiment with different signal chain configurations, placing effects such as distortion, overdrive, and modulation before or after the amp model to achieve different tonal effects and textures.

5. Pay Attention to Mic Placement: When using microphone and cabinet modeling options in the studio, pay close attention to mic placement to achieve the best possible tone and recording quality. Experiment with different mic positions relative to the speaker cone, as well as different mic models and cabinet simulations, to capture the

desired sound and achieve optimal realism and clarity in your recordings.

6. Practice Good Gain Staging: Maintain good gain staging throughout your signal chain to prevent noise, distortion, and other unwanted artifacts from degrading your tone and recording quality. Keep input levels consistent and avoid excessive gain or volume settings that can lead to clipping and distortion in your recordings.

7. Monitor Your Levels: Keep an eye on your levels during live performances and studio recordings to ensure that your signal remains clean and distortion-free. Use the Tone Master Pro's built-in meters and monitoring tools to monitor input and output levels, adjusting gain settings as needed to achieve optimal signal-to-noise ratio and dynamic range.

8. Experiment with Room Acoustics: In studio recording settings, experiment with different room acoustics and mic placements to capture the desired ambience and spatial characteristics in your recordings. Consider using acoustic treatment and isolation techniques to minimize reflections and background noise, creating a clean and controlled

recording environment that enhances the clarity and realism of your guitar tone.

By following these tips for optimal performance and recording quality with the Tone Master Pro, you can unlock the full potential of this versatile amp and achieve professional-level results in both live and studio settings. Experimentation, attention to detail, and a willingness to explore new sounds and techniques are key to getting the most out of your Tone Master Pro and elevating your guitar playing to new heights.

Chapter 7: Tips and Tricks

Expert Tips for Maximizing Sound Quality

Maximizing sound quality with the Fender Tone Master Pro requires a combination of technical understanding, attention to detail, and a keen ear for tone. Let's delve into expert tips to help you achieve the best possible sound quality from your Tone Master Pro in both live performance and studio recording settings.

1. Invest in Quality Cables and Connections: Sound quality starts with the cables and connections you use to connect your guitar, pedals, and Tone Master Pro. Invest in high-quality instrument cables with durable connectors to minimize signal loss and interference, ensuring clean and clear sound transmission from your guitar to the amp.

2. Optimize Your Guitar Setup: A well-maintained and properly set up guitar can significantly impact sound quality. Ensure that your guitar is properly intonated, with fresh strings and optimal action height, to achieve the best possible tone and playability. Experiment with different pickups and pickup settings to find the perfect balance of warmth, clarity, and dynamics for your playing style.

3. Master the EQ Controls: Understanding how to effectively use the EQ controls on the Tone Master Pro is essential for shaping your tone and achieving optimal sound quality. Experiment with different EQ settings to boost or cut specific frequencies, sculpting your tone to fit the musical context and achieve clarity, definition, and balance in your sound.

4. Fine-Tune Your Effects: Take the time to fine-tune your effects settings to achieve the desired sound and texture for each song and performance scenario. Experiment with different effect combinations, parameter settings, and intensity levels to add depth, dimension, and character to your tone, while ensuring that effects do not overpower the natural sound of your guitar.

5. Pay Attention to Volume and Gain: Maintaining optimal volume and gain levels is crucial for achieving clean, distortion-free sound quality with the Tone Master Pro. Avoid excessive volume or gain settings that can lead to clipping, distortion, and unwanted artifacts in your tone. Use the Tone Master Pro's built-in volume and gain controls to adjust levels dynamically, ensuring that your tone remains balanced and consistent throughout your performance or recording session.

6. Experiment with Mic Placement: When using microphone and cabinet modeling options in the studio, experiment with different mic placements to capture the best possible tone and recording quality. Move the virtual microphone around the speaker cone to find the sweet spot that enhances the natural characteristics of your guitar tone, while minimizing unwanted resonance and coloration.

7. Monitor Your Signal Chain: Pay close attention to your signal chain and monitor each component for any issues or anomalies that may affect sound quality. Check for loose connections, faulty cables, and other potential sources of noise or interference that can degrade your tone. Use the Tone Master Pro's built-in meters and monitoring tools to keep track of input and output levels, ensuring optimal signal-to-noise ratio and dynamic range.

8. Practice Good Room Acoustics: In studio recording settings, consider the acoustics of your recording environment and implement acoustic treatment and isolation techniques to minimize reflections, reverberation, and background noise. Create a clean and controlled recording space that enhances the clarity, realism, and fidelity of your guitar tone, allowing you to capture professional-quality recordings with ease.

By following these expert tips for maximizing sound quality with the Fender Tone Master Pro, you can unlock the full potential of this versatile amp and achieve professional-level results in both live performance and studio recording settings. Experimentation, attention to detail, and a commitment to excellence are key to achieving the best possible sound quality with your Tone Master Pro and elevating your guitar playing to new heights.

Creative Ways to Use the Tone Master Pro

The Fender Tone Master Pro is not just a tool for replicating classic guitar tones; it's a versatile platform for creativity and exploration. Here, we'll explore several creative ways to use the Tone Master Pro to expand your sonic palette and inspire new musical ideas.

1. Layered Soundscapes: Experiment with layering multiple guitar tracks using the Tone Master Pro to create lush, textured soundscapes. Utilize different amp models, effects, and EQ settings for each track to achieve a rich, dynamic blend of tones that can serve as the foundation for ambient compositions, film scores, or experimental music projects. Use the Tone Master Pro's stereo outputs to create wide, immersive stereo imaging, further enhancing the depth and complexity of your soundscapes.

2. Hybrid Instrumentation: Explore the possibility of incorporating non-guitar instruments into your Tone Master Pro setup to create unique hybrid sounds. Connect synthesizers, drum machines, or other electronic instruments to the Tone Master Pro's auxiliary inputs or effects loops, blending analog and digital elements to create innovative sonic textures and timbres. Experiment with signal routing, effects processing, and performance techniques to blur the boundaries between traditional and electronic instrumentation, opening up new avenues for musical expression.

3. Live Looping: Take advantage of the Tone Master Pro's built-in looper to create live loops and layers in real-time. Use the looper to capture and manipulate guitar phrases, chord progressions, and melodic motifs, building intricate arrangements on the fly. Experiment with overdubbing, layering, and phrase manipulation to create dynamic, evolving musical landscapes that can serve as the basis for improvisation, composition, or live performance.

4. Experimental Effects Processing: Push the boundaries of conventional guitar effects processing by experimenting with unconventional signal chains, feedback loops, and audio manipulation techniques. Use the Tone Master Pro's extensive

effects routing options to create complex, evolving soundscapes that blur the line between guitar and synthesis. Explore techniques such as granular synthesis, spectral processing, and stochastic modulation to create otherworldly textures and timbres that defy categorization.

5. Interactive Performance Art: Use the Tone Master Pro as a tool for interactive performance art, incorporating visual elements, movement, and audience participation into your live performances. Experiment with live video projection, interactive lighting, and sensor-based controllers to create immersive, multi-sensory experiences that engage and captivate audiences. Use the Tone Master Pro's versatility and flexibility to adapt to different performance contexts and venues, from intimate gallery spaces to large-scale festivals.

6. Collaborative Composition: Collaborate with other musicians, artists, and performers to create collaborative compositions and multimedia projects using the Tone Master Pro as a central hub. Use the Tone Master Pro's built-in audio interface and MIDI capabilities to synchronize multiple instruments, controllers, and software applications, allowing for seamless integration and communication between different elements of the

composition. Experiment with real-time improvisation, collective improvisation, and generative music techniques to create spontaneous, organic compositions that evolve and unfold in unpredictable ways.

7. Educational Tool: Use the Tone Master Pro as an educational tool to teach music theory, composition, and performance techniques. Explore different musical genres, styles, and traditions using the Tone Master Pro's vast library of amp models, effects, and presets. Use the Tone Master Pro's intuitive interface and real-time feedback to demonstrate concepts such as signal processing, sound design, and live performance, providing students with hands-on experience and practical skills that can be applied in a variety of musical contexts.

By exploring these creative ways to use the Tone Master Pro, you can unlock new possibilities for musical expression, experimentation, and collaboration. Whether you're a seasoned musician, a budding artist, or an educator looking to inspire the next generation of musicians, the Tone Master Pro offers endless opportunities for creativity and innovation. Experiment, explore, and let your imagination run wild—the possibilities are limitless.

Chapter 8: Troubleshooting and Maintenance

Common Issues and Solutions

While the Fender Tone Master Pro is a powerful and versatile guitar amp, like any piece of equipment, it can encounter common issues that may affect its performance. In this chapter, we'll explore some of these issues and provide solutions to help troubleshoot and resolve them effectively.

1. No Power or Sound Output: If your Tone Master Pro is not powering on or producing sound, the first step is to check the power source and connections. Ensure that the power cable is securely plugged into a functioning power outlet and that the power switch on the amp is in the "on" position. If the amp still does not power on, check the fuse and replace it if necessary. If there is still no sound output, check the guitar cable, input jack, and volume settings on the amp to ensure proper connectivity.

2. Intermittent Sound or Noise Issues: If you're experiencing intermittent sound or noise issues with your Tone Master Pro, the problem may be related to faulty cables, loose connections, or interference from other electronic devices. Check all cables and connections for any signs of damage or wear, and replace any cables that appear damaged. Ensure that the amp is properly grounded and that there are no sources of electromagnetic interference nearby, such as cell phones, Wi-Fi routers, or fluorescent lights.

3. Tone or EQ Settings Not Responding: If the tone or EQ settings on your Tone Master Pro are not responding as expected, the issue may be related to software or firmware updates. Check the Fender website for any available updates or patches for the Tone Master Pro, and follow the instructions to install them. If the problem persists, perform a factory reset on the amp to restore it to its default settings and see if that resolves the issue.

4. Effects Not Working Properly: If the effects on your Tone Master Pro are not working properly, check the settings and connections for each effect to ensure they are configured correctly. Make sure that the effects loop is enabled and that all pedals and external effects devices are properly connected to the amp. If certain effects are still not functioning as expected, try bypassing them individually to identify any faulty pedals or cables that may be causing the issue.

5. Overheating or Thermal Shutdown: If your Tone Master Pro is overheating or experiencing thermal shutdown, the issue may be related to prolonged use at high volume levels or in hot environments. To prevent overheating, ensure that the amp is properly ventilated and that airflow is not obstructed by any objects or debris. Reduce the volume level or take breaks between extended periods of use to allow the amp to cool down. If the problem persists, consult a professional technician for further assistance.

6. Software or Firmware Errors: If you encounter software or firmware errors with your Tone Master Pro, such as freezes, crashes, or glitches, try performing a factory reset to restore the amp to its default settings. If the problem persists, contact Fender customer support for assistance and inquire about any available software updates or troubleshooting tips.

7. Physical Damage or Wear: If your Tone Master Pro has sustained physical damage or shows signs of wear and tear, such as dents, scratches, or loose components, it may affect its performance. Inspect the amp carefully for any visible damage and address any issues promptly to prevent further damage or malfunctions. If necessary, consult a professional technician for repairs or maintenance to ensure the long-term reliability and performance of your Tone Master Pro.

By addressing these common issues and implementing the corresponding solutions, you can troubleshoot and resolve any problems that may arise with your Fender Tone Master Pro, ensuring optimal performance and reliability for your guitar playing needs. Remember to always follow proper safety precautions and consult a professional technician if you encounter any issues that cannot be resolved through basic troubleshooting methods.

Care and Maintenance Guidelines

Proper care and maintenance of your Fender Tone Master Pro are essential for ensuring optimal performance, longevity, and reliability. In this section, we'll provide comprehensive guidelines to help you keep your amp in top condition and preserve its sound quality for years to come.

1. Cleaning and Dusting: Regularly clean and dust your Tone Master Pro to prevent the buildup of dirt, dust, and debris that can affect its appearance and performance. Use a soft, dry cloth to gently wipe down the exterior surfaces of the amp, including the control knobs, touchscreen, and input/output jacks. Avoid using harsh chemicals or abrasive cleaners that may damage the finish or components of the amp.

2. Ventilation and Airflow: Ensure proper ventilation and airflow around your Tone Master Pro to prevent overheating and thermal shutdown. Place the amp in a well-ventilated area with adequate space around it to allow for airflow and heat dissipation. Avoid placing the amp near heat sources, such as radiators or heating vents, that may cause it to overheat.

3. Storage and Transportation: When not in use, store your Tone Master Pro in a safe and secure location to protect it from damage and environmental hazards. Use a protective cover or case to shield the amp from dust, moisture, and

impact during storage and transportation. Avoid exposing the amp to extreme temperatures or humidity levels that may cause damage to its components or finish.

4. Tube Replacement: Unlike traditional tube amps, the Tone Master Pro does not require tube replacement or maintenance. However, if you encounter any issues with the amp's performance, such as distorted sound or noise issues, consult a professional technician for diagnosis and repair.

5. Software and Firmware Updates: Stay up to date with the latest software and firmware updates for your Tone Master Pro to ensure optimal performance and compatibility with other devices and software applications. Check the Fender website regularly for any available updates or patches, and follow the instructions to install them correctly.

6. Input and Output Jacks: Inspect the input and output jacks on your Tone Master Pro regularly for any signs of damage or wear, such as loose connections or corrosion. Clean the jacks with a soft, dry cloth to remove any dirt or debris that may affect their performance. Avoid using excessive

force when plugging in cables to prevent damage to the jacks or connectors.

7. Power Supply and Cables: Check the power supply and cables for your Tone Master Pro periodically to ensure they are in good condition and free from damage or wear. Replace any damaged or frayed cables immediately to prevent electrical hazards or malfunctions. Use high-quality cables and connectors to ensure reliable power delivery and signal transmission to your amp.

8. Professional Inspection and Maintenance: If you encounter any issues with your Tone Master Pro that cannot be resolved through basic troubleshooting methods, consult a professional technician for inspection and maintenance. Professional technicians have the expertise and tools to diagnose and repair complex issues with your amp, ensuring optimal performance and reliability.

By following these care and maintenance guidelines, you can keep your Fender Tone Master Pro in top condition and enjoy years of reliable performance and pristine sound quality. Remember to always handle your amp with care, avoid exposing it to harsh environmental conditions, and address any issues promptly to prevent further damage or malfunctions. With proper care and maintenance, your Tone Master Pro will continue to deliver exceptional tone and performance for years to come.

Conclusion

As we conclude our exploration of the Fender Tone Master Pro, it's essential to reflect on its capabilities, performance, and overall value. Throughout this user guide, we've delved into various aspects of the Tone Master Pro, from its intuitive interface and extensive amp models to its versatile effects and advanced features. Now, let's summarize our final thoughts and recommendations for this innovative digital modeling amp.

First and foremost, the Fender Tone Master Pro stands out for its exceptional sound quality, ease of use, and versatility. With its vast library of classic amp models, authentic effects, and customizable presets, the Tone Master Pro offers guitarists an unparalleled level of flexibility and control over their tone. Whether you're a seasoned professional or an aspiring musician, the Tone Master Pro provides a platform for creativity and expression that is second to none.

One of the standout features of the Tone Master Pro is its intuitive interface, which allows users to navigate seamlessly through amp models, effects, and settings with ease. The touchscreen display, foot switches, and knobs provide tactile control over every aspect of the amp's sound, making it easy to dial in the perfect tone for any musical style or genre. Additionally, the Tone Master Pro's built-in audio interface and MIDI capabilities open up a world of possibilities for recording, performance, and collaboration, making it a valuable tool for both studio and stage.

In terms of performance, the Tone Master Pro delivers in spades. Whether you're jamming in your bedroom, rehearsing with your band, or playing live on stage, the Tone Master Pro offers the power, clarity, and responsiveness that guitarists demand. From pristine clean tones to searing overdrive and everything in between, the Tone Master Pro faithfully recreates the classic Fender sound with precision and authenticity.

Furthermore, the Tone Master Pro's robust construction and durable components ensure reliable performance and long-term durability, even under demanding conditions. Whether you're gigging regularly or recording in the studio, you can count on the Tone Master Pro to deliver consistent, high-quality sound, night after night.

In terms of recommendations, the Fender Tone Master Pro is an excellent choice for guitarists seeking a versatile, reliable, and feature-rich amp for both live performance and studio recording. Its combination of classic Fender tones, modern digital technology, and intuitive design make it a standout option in the crowded field of digital modeling amps.

For those who value portability and convenience, the Tone Master Pro's compact size and lightweight design make it easy to transport and set up wherever you go. Whether you're playing small club gigs, recording sessions, or jamming at home, the Tone Master Pro is a versatile and reliable companion that delivers exceptional tone and performance, every time.

The Fender Tone Master Pro is a game-changer in the world of guitar amplification. With its authentic tones, intuitive interface, and versatile features, the Tone Master Pro offers guitarists a powerful tool for unlocking their creative potential and taking their playing to new heights. Whether you're a seasoned professional or an aspiring musician, the Tone Master Pro is sure to inspire and delight with its exceptional sound quality and performance.